30 WEEK BIBLE STUDY FOR TEEN GIRLS

Queen in the Making

30 Week Bible Study for Teen Girls

Leader's Guide

30 WEEK BIBLE STUDY FOR TEEN GIRLS

Queen in the Making

30 Week Bible Study for Teen Girls

Leader's Guide

By
Reverend Onedia N. Gage, Ph. D.

Library of Congress

Queen in the Making:

30 Week Bible Study for Teen Girls

Leader's Guide

All Rights Reserved © 2018
Rev. Onedia N. Gage

No part of this of book may be reproduced or transmitted in
Any form or by any means, graphic, electronic, or mechanical,
Including photocopying, recording, taping, or by any
Information storage or retrieval system, without the
Permission in writing from the publisher.

Purple Ink, Inc. Press

For Information:
Purple Ink, Inc.
P O Box 300113
Houston, TX 77230

www.purpleink.net ♦ www.onediagage.com

onediagage@purpleink.net ♦ onediagage@onediagage.com

ISBN:

978-1-939119-68-1

Printed in United States

Other Books by
Reverend Onedia N. Gage, Ph. D.

90 Days of Powerful Words: Affirmations & Advice for Girls
Are You Ready for 9th Grade . . . Again? A Family's Guide to Success
As We Grow Together Daily Devotional for Expectant Couples
As We Grow Together Prayer Journal for Expectant Couples
As We Grow Together Bible Study: Her Workbook
As We Grow Together Bible Study: His Workbook
The Best 40 Days of My Life: A Journey of Spiritual Renewal
The Blue Print: Poetry for the Soul
From Fat to Fit in 90 Days: A Fitness Journal
From Two to One: The Notebook for the Christian Couple
Hannah's Voice: Powerful Lessons in Prayer
Her Story: Bible Study
Her Story: The Devotional
Her Story: The Legacy Journal
Her Story: Prayers and Journal
ILY! A Mother Daughter Relationship Workbook
In Her Own Words: Notebook for the Christian Woman
In Purple Ink: Poetry for the Spirit
Intensive Couples Retreat: Her Workbook
Intensive Couples Retreat: His Workbook
Living A Whole Life: Sermons Which Provide, Prompt, and Promote Life
Love Letters to God from a Teenage Girl
The Measure of a Woman: The Details of Her Soul
The Notebook: For Me, About Me, By Me
The Notebook for the Christian Teen
On This Journey Daily Devotional for Young People
On This Journey Prayer Journal for Young People
On This Journey Prayer Journal for Young People, Vol. 2
One Day More Than We Deserve Prayer Journal for the Growing Christian
Promises, Promises: A Christian Novel
Queen in the Making: 30 Week Bible Study for Teen Girls
She Spoke Volumes . . . And Then Some
Six Months of Solitude: The Sanctity of Singleness Notebook
There's a Queen Inside: Lessons in Being a Great Girl
Tools for These Times: Timely Sermons for Uncertain Times
With An Anointed Voice: The Power of Prayer

30 WEEK BIBLE STUDY FOR TEEN GIRLS

Yielded and Submitted: A Woman's Journey for a Life Dedicated to God
Yielded and Submitted: A Woman's Journey for a Life Dedicated to God An Intimate Study
Yielded and Submitted: A Woman's Journey for a Life Dedicated to God Prayers and Journal

Dedication

To My Queen in the Making, Hillary!

To the Queens in the Making who I serve

Actively and passively,

Up close and from a distance.

To the Mothers and Fathers of those

Queens in the Making

Thank you for letting me impact her life!

30 WEEK BIBLE STUDY FOR TEEN GIRLS

God's Words

Deuteronomy 6:5 (NIV)

⁵ Love the LORD your God with all your heart and with all your soul and with all your strength.

Psalm 139:14 (NIV)

¹⁴ I praise You because I am fearfully and wonderfully made;
   Your works are wonderful,
   I know that full well.

Jeremiah 1:5 (NIV)

⁵ "Before I formed you in the womb I knew you,
   before you were born I set you apart;
   I appointed you as a prophet to the nations."

30 WEEK BIBLE STUDY FOR TEEN GIRLS

Dear God,

Thank You for making me a girl! Thank You for Your provisions for me and Your other daughters. For You to love us the way that You do is amazing! Thank You for validating us and giving us work to do. Thank You for calling us Your daughters.

Thank You for Your compassion, leadership, plans, forgiveness, and wisdom. Lord, I want You to be proud of me and I hope that I don't disappoint You as much as I previously had. Help me to overcome temptation. Help me to hear from You and discern Your voice. Help me to be obedient to Your urgings and Your will.

Thank You for Jesus and the Holy Spirit. I need an intercessor and You have sent one to me. Thank You for creating me. Thank You for the plans that You have for my life.

Thank You for helping us girls to survive a world that does not really embrace us the way You created us. They make it difficult to be a girl. Help us to continue to be faithful. Create in us a clean heart. Help us to keep the faith which we need to have a great relationship with You.

Thank You for empowering us to be powerful and wonderful. Thank You for making us fearfully and wonderfully.

Thank You for this book and these girls it will serve. Thank You for using me to complete Your work.

I pray for these blessings in Jesus' name.

Amen

30 WEEK BIBLE STUDY FOR TEEN GIRLS

Dear Facilitator/Ministry Leader:

For every girl we meet in church or at camp or at school or wherever, that girl needs us to be the intercessor, the leader, the adult, the guidance, the sounding board, the listening ear, and the advice giver. She does not need, nor should she expect us to be her friend.

This study is designed to help her navigate the toughest areas of her life. She looks up to you: she watches you. You mentor her—initially without your knowledge. You influence her without your knowledge or consent. You change her mind and sometimes her heart, and certainly her behavior all because she has been in your presence.

Study. Pray. Fast. Meditate. She depends on your attention to God. She needs your total dependency on God.

Show her what you know. Share with her your story so that she may understand that what she is experiencing is not new and is survivable. Remind her that God does not make any mistakes and she is a plan for which God has a purpose.

Engage her at a HIGH level! She needs a level voice to counteract the voice of the internet and her friends who also gather their information from the biased internet. She needs affirmation and reminders of her purpose and His calling on her life.

Be careful! What you teach, you will be held accountable for as well. You will have to espouse and embrace these lessons. You will be convicted in the areas where you have avoided God.

She needs your help. She needs your love. She needs your protection. She needs your patience. She needs your forgiveness. She needs your permission to forgive herself. She needs your full and undivided attention. She does not know how to ask for your attention, but she desperately needs it.

I am praying for you. You will need to fast and pray regularly on her behalf.

Thank you for serving her and not avoiding her.

In God's Service,

Reverend Onedia N. Gage

30 WEEK BIBLE STUDY FOR TEEN GIRLS

Dear Parents:

I pray your strength in the Lord through these lessons. I have had some of the most enlightening experiences by teaching young ladies about God, life and her future.

I have only an inkling of what your journey has been like. I actually have no idea of what your journey has been like, however, I do know that your journey is not new and it is not the first or last time a parent will have that same experience.

Take refuge in God in this season. Keep in mind that God is in complete control! God also knows your circumstances and your situations. God has not forgotten you and your tears and your prayers.

God is clear about what you stand in need of. God also hears your prayers and knows the desires of your heart.

Help her through this 30-week study. She needs your prayers, support, and guidance. Feel free to submit your prayer requests to me via phone, text, email or by mail.

Likewise, I am convinced that as parents, we need each other. I also authorize you to actively act like those older parents did before us, where we did not have any privacy: go through her phone, read the messages, view the pictures, check the internet browsing history, know her passwords, keep tabs on her friends, ask questions of her about the details of her daily life, require her to come home at a curfew, teach her the manners she needs to survive in this world, require her to have standards for the life you dream of for her and remember you are the parent and consequently, you have the last word. Moreover, by all means, take the bedroom door off its hinges if you cannot get the door open or if you cannot get her out of her room or otherwise get her attention.

You have exactly 6,574 days to turn her into a queen from your little girl. Use this time wisely. These days seem like a long time but if you are not careful, they will pass you by. Keep in mind that you are first in line as her source for information, the person who can influence her, and the orchestrator of her spiritual foundation. This time requires your full attention.

Be a bold, courageous parent!

She needs you to be bold and courageous in order for her to be a Queen!

Just trying to parent a Queen in the Making too,

Reverend Onedia N. Gage

30 WEEK BIBLE STUDY FOR TEEN GIRLS

Table of Contents

Dedication		9
Scripture		11
Prayer		13
Letters		15
The Study		23
Week One:	Who Is God? Who Does He Day That You Are?	25
Week Two:	God Loves You Extravagantly	29
Week Three:	God Created You on Purpose, With a Purpose, To Be a Purpose	33
Week Four:	God Forgives You	37
Week Five:	God Hears You—Pray!	40
Week Six:	God Expects Faith	44
Week Seven:	God Gifts You	48
Week Eight:	Sex and Intimate Relationships	52
Week Nine:	God Gives Wisdom Through Experience Because You Asked	56
Week Ten:	God Requires Study and Meditation	60
Week Eleven:	In Times of Trouble	64
Week Twelve:	Follow the One Who Counts: Jesus	67
Week Thirteen:	Parents	78

30 WEEK BIBLE STUDY FOR TEEN GIRLS

Week Fourteen:	Ruth: Persist for What is Right	84
Week Fifteen:	Grace and Mercy Defined	89
Week Sixteen:	Eve: To Whom Much is Required	92
Week Seventeen:	Martha: A Bad Attitude and Wrong Motives	96
Week Eighteen:	Naomi: Transparency and Direction	101
Week Nineteen:	Esther: "Overcoming your position"	104
Week Twenty:	Hannah: "A Prayer Warrior—Transparent and Unwavering"	109
Week Twenty-One:	Bathsheba: Situational Sin	113
Week Twenty-Two:	Lois and Eunice: A Legacy of Faith	117
Week Twenty-Three:	Lydia: Sharing Jesus with Others	122
Week Twenty-Four:	Mary: A Life Worthy of Being Chosen	126
Week Twenty-Five:	The Issue of Blood: A Dogmatic Perseverance and Without Issue of Image	130
Week Twenty-Six:	Work Ethic	134
Week Twenty-Seven:	With Zeal, Pursue and Proceed	138
Week Twenty-Eight:	Weapons for Warfare	143
Week Twenty-Nine:	God Made You a Girl	146
Week Thirty:	How Today Effects Your Future	150
Appendix		155
Acknowledgements		157
About the Queen		159

THE NERVE TO DREAM

By Onedia N. Gage

You have the nerve to dream
And expect others to do the same
The audacity

You know dreams don't come true
You know that we don't leave our circumstances
You know that we cannot convince others to believe falsely

You have the nerve and the audacity
To expect us to dream
When there is blight and slums and
Economic hardships

You still dream for better than we have it
Better than <u>all</u> our ancestors
We have more educated
We have more educators
We have more leaders
We have more politicians
We have more wealthy
We have more
. . . yet you still dream of more

You dream that still more can happen
The audacity of you
And the nerve
And the gall of
You to tell our children that they
Can have more than we have
Define more
How much more

30 WEEK BIBLE STUDY FOR TEEN GIRLS

More with what?
Less?

Dreams.
You still do it
And in the worst of times
By perception
By the naked eye
But up close they deserve every opportunity to dream
They deserve hopes
They deserve dreams
They deserve the audacity to look at me and
<u>Know</u> that they too can have what we have
And have more of it.

You still dream.

Reprinted from **In Purple Ink: Poetry for the Spirit**

Queen In The Making

30 Week Bible Study for Teen Girls

Leader's Guide

30 WEEK BIBLE STUDY FOR TEEN GIRLS

WEEK ONE

Who is God?

Who does He say that you are?

Genesis 1:1-31

Class Agenda:

Class Introductions

    Introduce yourself.

    Why are you in this study?

    Who made you come?

    What do you hope to gain from this study?

Read the letter "Dear Girl" to the class

Read the Scripture	5 attendees
Pray	1 attendee
The Covenant of the Study	Leader starts, attendees read the next portions

    They all sign it each other's covenant

Narrative Discussion:

"What were the most important points of the narrative?" Discuss those points.

30 WEEK BIBLE STUDY FOR TEEN GIRLS

Reflection Question Discussion:

As you ask these questions, allow 1-2 responses for each question. They need to time to reflect and share with each other. This is a long study. They will need to build trust and community amongst each other.

"What was the hardest question to answer in the reflection questions? Why?"

"What was the most thought-provoking question in the reflection questions? Why? Did you share the question with anyone?"

"What question caused you the most concern?"

"Did you have any questions after the study? What were the questions?"

Project Discussion:

The Mirror: "How did your mirror come together?"

"What happened when you looked at yourself in the mirror for the first time without criticizing yourself?"

"Were you able to do it the first time? How many times did it take to become comfortable with looking at yourself without a critical thought?"

"How did looking at yourself without criticism make you feel?"

"What did you learn about yourself from week 1?"

"What was the most important detail of your journal?"

Close with a testimony about when you first met God. (Yours or an QIM.)

Answer any questions.

Next week's assignment.

Pray.

WEEK ONE REFLECTION

1. What do you know about God? Who first told you about God?

   _____

   _____

2. What do you think God thinks of you? What do you think of yourself? What do others think of you? Why does that matter?

   _____

   _____

3. How does someone else's opinion of you cause you to change how you feel about yourself? Why do they have that much influence over your opinion of yourself?

   _____

   _____

4. How do you think that your character and image, details of your mind and your heart, and most importantly, your soul were designed?

   _____

   _____

5. What does it take to upgrade your image of yourself, and consequently, your image in the presence of others?

   _____

   _____

6. Why does your image matter? Who do you really represent: yourself, your parents/family, God? What behavior exhibits the best representation of who you really represent?

30 WEEK BIBLE STUDY FOR TEEN GIRLS

_____

_____

7. What do you need to change so that you are properly representing the God who loves you and who keeps you?

_____

_____

8. When you look at yourself in the mirror, do you look at yourself with criticism or disdain? Try to look at the image that God sees. What do you see?

_____

_____

WEEK TWO

God Loves You Extravagantly

John 3:16 (NIV)

1 Corinthians 13:13 (MSG)

Read the Scripture	2 attendees
Pray	1 attendee
The Covenant of the Study	Leader reminds of the covenant

Narrative Discussion:

"What were the most important points of the narrative?" Discuss those points.

Reflection Question Discussion:

As you ask these questions, allow 1-2 responses for each question. They need to time to reflect and share with each other. This is a long study. They will need to build trust and community amongst each other.

"What was the hardest question to answer in the reflection questions? Why?"

"What was the most thought-provoking question in the reflection questions? Why? Did you share the question with anyone?"

"What question caused you the most concern?"

"Did you have any questions after the study? What were the questions?"

Project Discussion:

"You had to write 4 letters. Which one was the most difficult to write?"

30 WEEK BIBLE STUDY FOR TEEN GIRLS

"Which one was the easiest?"

"What did you learn about yourself from week 2?"

"What was the most important detail of your journal?"

Close with a testimony when you felt God's love enough to share the experience with others. (Leader or QIM).

Answer any questions.

Next week's assignment.

Pray.

WEEK TWO REFLECTION

1. Define love. God's definition. Your definition. The world's definition. What is the major difference between those definitions?

   _____
   _____

2. What does it take to love others? Is it difficult? Why? What happened?

   _____
   _____

3. Why are you rejecting love?

   _____
   _____

4. Do you feel unlovable? Why or why not?

   _____
   _____

5. Who loves you? Why do they love you? How do you know?

   _____
   _____

6. What do you do to love others? How do they know that you love them?

   _____
   _____

7. Does love cost or is it free? Is it real love if it costs something? Explain.

_____

_____

8. Do you love certain people differently than others? Who? Why?

_____

_____

9. How do you feel when you know that you are loved? Unconditional love?

_____

_____

10. Do you think you need permission to love yourself? Why? Do you need permission to love someone else? Why?

_____

_____

WEEK THREE

God created you on purpose, with a purpose,

To be a purpose

Jeremiah 1:5

Jeremiah 29:11

Read the Scripture	5 attendees
Pray	1 attendee
The Covenant of the Study	Leader reminds of the covenant

Narrative Discussion:

"What were the most important points of the narrative?" Discuss those points.

Reflection Question Discussion:

As you ask these questions, allow 1-2 responses for each question. They need to time to reflect and share with each other. This is a long study. They will need to build trust and community amongst each other.

"What was the hardest question to answer in the reflection questions? Why?"

"What was the most thought-provoking question in the reflection questions? Why? Did you share the question with anyone?"

"What question caused you the most concern?"

"Did you have any questions after the study? What were the questions?"

Project Discussion:

30 WEEK BIBLE STUDY FOR TEEN GIRLS

"What is the most important part of your vision board?"

"What did you learn about yourself from week 3?"

"What was the most important detail of your journal?"

Close with a testimony about when you first realized the purpose God gave you. (Yours or an QIM.)

Answer any questions.

Next week's assignment.

Pray.

WEEK THREE REFLECTION

1. What do you think about the scriptures? What do they mean to you?

_____
_____

2. How did these scriptures change your thoughts and attitude about yourself?

_____
_____

3. Did this help you to reconsider the negative perception you had about yourself previously? How will your perception about yourself change?

_____
_____

4. Who are the negative people who need to be removed from your head?

_____
_____

5. What is your purpose? What do you want to be as an adult?

_____
_____

6. What are your dreams?

_____
_____

30 WEEK BIBLE STUDY FOR TEEN GIRLS

7. What do you think God wants you to do? How will you find out?

_____

_____

8. Who helps you to be positive and optimistic about your life? What does that person do? Why?

_____

_____

WEEK FOUR

God Forgives You

Colossians 3:13

Mark 11:25

1 John 1:9

Read the Scripture — 3 attendees

Pray — 1 attendee

The Covenant of the Study — "What this mean to you?"

Narrative Discussion:

"What were the most important points of the narrative?" Discuss those points.

Reflection Question Discussion:

As you ask these questions, allow 1-2 responses for each question. They need to time to reflect and share with each other. This is a long study. They will need to build trust and community amongst each other.

"What was the hardest question to answer in the reflection questions? Why?"

"What was the most thought-provoking question in the reflection questions? Why? Did you share the question with anyone?"

"What question caused you the most concern?"

"Did you have any questions after the study? What were the questions?"

Project Discussion:

30 WEEK BIBLE STUDY FOR TEEN GIRLS

"Among the four letters, which one was the easiest? Why?"

"Among the four letters, which one was the most difficult to write? Why?"

"What did you learn about yourself from week 4?"

"What was the most important detail of your journal?"

Close with a testimony about when you first realized that God had forgiven you. (Yours or an QIM.)

Answer any questions.

Next week's assignment.

Pray.

WEEK FOUR REFLECTION

1. Who do you need to forgive? Make a two-column list with the name of the person and the reason why you need to forgive them.

___

___

2. What do you need to be forgiven by God? By yourself?

___

___

3. What can you do to avoid needing forgiveness?

___

___

4. Who do you need to be forgiven by? How will you go about securing that forgiveness?

___

___

WEEK FIVE

God Hears You

Pray

Matthew 6:9-14

Matthew 5:44

Luke 6:28

James 5:18

Read the Scripture	4 attendees
Pray	1 attendee
The Covenant of the Study	"How does this translate into the life you lead?"

Narrative Discussion:

"What were the most important points of the narrative?" Discuss those points.

Reflection Question Discussion:

As you ask these questions, allow 1-2 responses for each question. They need to time to reflect and share with each other. This is a long study. They will need to build trust and community amongst each other.

"What was the hardest question to answer in the reflection questions? Why?"

"What was the most thought-provoking question in the reflection questions? Why? Did you share the question with anyone?"

"What question caused you the most concern?"

"Did you have any questions after the study? What were the questions?"

Project Discussion:

"What does it take for God to hear you?"

"What does it take it pray?"

"What did you learn about yourself from week 5?"

"What was the most important detail of your journal?"

Close with a testimony about when you first prayed to God. (Yours or an QIM.)

Answer any questions.

Next week's assignment.

Pray.

WEEK FIVE REFLECTION

1. Who do you know that prays? Can you talk to them about their prayer life? Ask her/him all about their prayer life, such as when, why, how, who, where and what.

_____

_____

2. Do you pray? Are there any specific conditions under which you pray or do not pray? Why do you pray?

_____

_____

3. Do you pray with others? Who? Under what conditions?

_____

_____

4. Are you afraid to pray? Why or why not?

_____

_____

5. Do you pray for others? Who? Why do you pray for them?

_____

_____

6. Do people pray for you? Who?

_____

_____

7. Why do you pray?

_____
_____

8. What stops you from praying?

_____
_____

9. What keeps you praying? Or what makes you stop?

_____
_____

10. What does prayer mean to you?

_____
_____

11. What age did you start recognizing prayer and its place in your life?

_____
_____

30 WEEK BIBLE STUDY FOR TEEN GIRLS

WEEK SIX

God Expects Faith

Hebrews 11:1-6 (KJV/NIV)

Read the Scripture	5 attendees
Pray	1 attendee
The Covenant of the Study	Remind about the covenant

Narrative Discussion:

"What were the most important points of the narrative?" Discuss those points.

Reflection Question Discussion:

As you ask these questions, allow 1-2 responses for each question. They need to time to reflect and share with each other. This is a long study. They will need to build trust and community amongst each other.

"What was the hardest question to answer in the reflection questions? Why?"

"What was the most thought-provoking question in the reflection questions? Why? Did you share the question with anyone?"

"What question caused you the most concern?"

"Did you have any questions after the study? What were the questions?"

Project Discussion:

"What did you learn about these letters in regard to faith?"

"What did you learn about yourself from week 6?"

"What was the most important detail of your journal?"

Close with a testimony about when you first realized that you had faith in God. (Yours or an QIM.)

Answer any questions.

Next week's assignment.

Pray.

30 WEEK BIBLE STUDY FOR TEEN GIRLS

WEEK SIX REFLECTION

1. Who do you know that has faith? How did you determine that they were faithful?

_____
_____

2. Do you consider yourself faithful?

_____
_____

3. What is your definition of faith?

_____
_____

4. Can you recall a time when you were faithful? Share the situation.

_____
_____

5. How will you improve your faithfulness?

_____
_____

6. Who will you share your faith with?

_____
_____

7. Who will you encourage to have faith?

8. How would God grade your faith?

9. Has there ever been a cost to your unfaithfulness?

10. Whose faith are you modeling your faith after?

30 WEEK BIBLE STUDY FOR TEEN GIRLS

WEEK SEVEN

God Gifts You

Romans 12:6-8

1 Corinthians 12:4-11

Read the Scripture	5 attendees
Pray	1 attendee
The Covenant of the Study	"How will you operate with a covenant in other areas of your life?"

Narrative Discussion:

"What were the most important points of the narrative?" Discuss those points.

Reflection Question Discussion:

As you ask these questions, allow 1-2 responses for each question. They need to time to reflect and share with each other. This is a long study. They will need to build trust and community amongst each other.

"What was the hardest question to answer in the reflection questions? Why?"

"What was the most thought-provoking question in the reflection questions? Why? Did you share the question with anyone?"

"What question caused you the most concern?"

"Did you have any questions after the study? What were the questions?"

Project Discussion:

"What did you learn about yourself from week 7?"

"What was the most important detail of your journal?"

Close with a testimony about when you first understood that God gifted you with something special. (Yours or an QIM.)

Answer any questions.

Next week's assignment.

Pray.

WEEK SEVEN REFLECTION

1. What are your gifts? What excuse(s) do you use to avoid being obedient? You do not know how God will multiply or manifest your gifts through your obedience.

   _____

   _____

2. What are your talents? What is your favorite gift of your gift(s)?

   _____

   _____

3. Why are you afraid to use your gifts and talents? When do you plan to use them for God as He intended?

   _____

   _____

4. What does God want you to do? How do you know? Why do you think God gave that gift/talent?

   _____

   _____

5. What will you do differently now that you know what your gifts are intended to do?

   _____

   _____

6. Who will you share with for gift mentoring? Who will you share your gifts with? Are you reluctant to share? Why? Are you scared to exercise your gift(s)? Why? How can we overcome that reluctancy and that fear?

   _____

7. What are your parent's gifts?

8. What friend(s) will you share about your gifts and theirs? What will you share? Do they know their gifts? Will you help them to discover their gifts?

30 WEEK BIBLE STUDY FOR TEEN GIRLS

WEEK EIGHT

Sex and Intimate Relationships

1 Corinthians 7:2

Read the Scripture   5 attendees

Pray   1 attendee

The Covenant of the Study   "Where else do you have a covenant?"

Narrative Discussion:

"What were the most important points of the narrative?" Discuss those points.

Reflection Question Discussion:

As you ask these questions, allow 1-2 responses for each question. They need to time to reflect and share with each other. This is a long study. They will need to build trust and community amongst each other.

"What was the hardest question to answer in the reflection questions? Why?"

"What was the most thought-provoking question in the reflection questions? Why? Did you share the question with anyone?"

"What question caused you the most concern?"

"Did you have any questions after the study? What were the questions?"

Project Discussion:

"What is the experience really worth?"

"Should you really do it before marriage?"

"What did you learn about yourself from week 8?"

"What was the most important detail of your journal?"

Close with a testimony about when you considered sex. What did you do to avoid having sex? (Yours or an QIM.)

Answer any questions.

Next week's assignment.

Pray.

30 WEEK BIBLE STUDY FOR TEEN GIRLS

WEEK EIGHT REFLECTION

1. What is sex as you define it?

   _____
   _____

2. Who do you know that is having sex? How long have they been having sex? How long have you known? Have they had more than one partner since they have been having sex?

   _____
   _____

3. Do you want to have sex? Why? Do your friends/media/others have a greater influence?

   _____
   _____

4. With whom do you want to have sex? Why? Does this person want to have sex with you?

   _____
   _____

5. When is an appropriate time to have sex? Can you wait until you are married to have sex? Why or why not?

   _____
   _____

6. Why is sex so important to you? To others? Why is it important right now?

   _____
   _____

7. When are you considering having sex? Today? Tomorrow? This week? Next week? Next month? Next 6 months? Next year?

_____

_____

8. What will it take for you to wait? What will it 'cost' for you to wait?

_____

_____

9. Why does the Bible say to wait until you are married to have sex?

_____

_____

10. What would you do if you became pregnant? Have the child? Abortion? Adoption? How long will that choice and consequence last? How will you endure/survive this consequence?

_____

_____

11. Do you know/understand that your parent(s) is graded on your behavior and outcome, so if you are pregnant or have the reputation for having sex, then it makes them look bad? Do you know/understand that they will be embarrassed? Do you know/understand that it will make them look like did not parent correctly?

_____

_____

12. Does how you feel about yourself—your self-esteem—determine your ability to say no to having sex?

_____

30 WEEK BIBLE STUDY FOR TEEN GIRLS

WEEK NINE

God Gives Wisdom Through Experience

Proverbs 1:1-7

Read the Scripture   2 attendees

Pray   1 attendee

The Covenant of the Study   "What does this mean to you?"

Narrative Discussion:

"What were the most important points of the narrative?" Discuss those points.

Reflection Question Discussion:

As you ask these questions, allow 1-2 responses for each question. They need to time to reflect and share with each other. This is a long study. They will need to build trust and community amongst each other.

"What was the hardest question to answer in the reflection questions? Why?"

"What was the most thought-provoking question in the reflection questions? Why? Did you share the question with anyone?"

"What question caused you the most concern?"

"Did you have any questions after the study? What were the questions?"

Project Discussion:

"What did you learn about yourself from week 9?"

"What was the most important detail of your journal?"

Close with a testimony about when you first discovered that you had wisdom. (Yours or an QIM.)

Answer any questions.

Next week's assignment.

Pray.

30 WEEK BIBLE STUDY FOR TEEN GIRLS

WEEK NINE REFLECTION

1. Define wisdom. How did you reach that definition?

_____

_____

2. Who do you know who is wise? When did you reach that decision?

_____

_____

3. When did you first ask to be wise?

_____

_____

4. Share three examples of when you have acted wisely.

_____

_____

5. Share three examples of when you acted without the benefit of wisdom, but the next time when the similar event happened, you responded wisely.

_____

_____

6. How do you share your wisdom with others?

_____

_____

7. Among your age group, who do you consider to be wise? Why?

_____

_____

8. List the top 10 scriptures listed as a result of a search for wisdom in biblegateway.com or the Bible on your phone. Read them. Select one that you can memorize.

_____

_____

30 WEEK BIBLE STUDY FOR TEEN GIRLS

WEEK TEN

Study and Meditation

Psalm 1

2 Timothy 2:15

Psalm 119:15

Read the Scripture	5 attendees
Pray	1 attendee
The Covenant of the Study	"How do you define covenant for others?"

Narrative Discussion:

"What were the most important points of the narrative?" Discuss those points.

Reflection Question Discussion:

As you ask these questions, allow 1-2 responses for each question. They need to time to reflect and share with each other. This is a long study. They will need to build trust and community amongst each other.

"What was the hardest question to answer in the reflection questions? Why?"

"What was the most thought-provoking question in the reflection questions? Why? Did you share the question with anyone?"

"What question caused you the most concern?"

"Did you have any questions after the study? What were the questions?"

Project Discussion:

Why do we think that is most impossible to wait until we are married?"

"What did you learn about yourself from week 10?"

"What was the most important detail of your journal?"

Close with a testimony about when you first heard from God. (Yours or an QIM.)

Answer any questions.

Next week's assignment.

Pray.

30 WEEK BIBLE STUDY FOR TEEN GIRLS

WEEK TEN REFLECTION

1. What time will you set aside to read God's word?

_____

_____

2. Do you have the Bible app on your phone so that you can read the Bible on the bus or other times when you are waiting?

_____

_____

3. Do you have a study partner or someone you can talk to about the Bible who is your age?

_____

_____

4. Do you have an adult/mentor who you can ask questions of about the Bible?

_____

_____

5. Do you know what a commentary is? Biblegateway.com has one that is useful.

_____

_____

6. What do you expect to gain by studying God's word?

_____

_____

7. What do you think will be the obstacle for studying and meditating? How will you overcome those obstacles?

_____

_____

30 WEEK BIBLE STUDY FOR TEEN GIRLS

WEEK ELEVEN

In Times of Trouble

2 Chronicle 7:14 (2 Chronicle 7:11-22)

Read the Scripture — 1 attendee

Pray — 1 attendee

The Covenant of the Study — "What does covenant mean in your life?"

Narrative Discussion:

"What were the most important points of the narrative?" Discuss those points.

Reflection Question Discussion:

As you ask these questions, allow 1-2 responses for each question. They need to time to reflect and share with each other. This is a long study. They will need to build trust and community amongst each other.

"What was the hardest question to answer in the reflection questions? Why?"

"What was the most thought-provoking question in the reflection questions? Why? Did you share the question with anyone?"

"What question caused you the most concern?"

"Did you have any questions after the study? What were the questions?"

Project Discussion:

"What did you learn from the meditation?"

"What did you learn about yourself from week 11?"

"What was the most important detail of your journal?"

Close with a testimony about when God saved you from trouble that you started. (Yours or an QIM.)

Answer any questions.

Next week's assignment.

Pray.

30 WEEK BIBLE STUDY FOR TEEN GIRLS

WEEK ELEVEN REFLECTION

1. How can you stay out of trouble? What will it take to stay out of trouble?

_____

_____

2. What are your 'go-to's'? Which one(s) will you need to eliminate or modify so that you do not increase the distance between you and God?

_____

_____

3. Can you seek God on all occasions? If not, when will you start?

_____

_____

WEEK TWELVE

Follow the One that Counts: Jesus

Leadership, Image, Reputation

Genesis 1:26-27

Matthew 6:25

Matthew 4:18-20

Romans 8:29	Luke 6:27-28
James 3:9-10	John 15:18
Luke 21:17 (13-17)	Matthew 14:29a (14:25-33)
Galatians 1:23-24	John 8:7

Read the Scripture	3 attendees
Pray	1 attendee
The Covenant of the Study	"What does covenant mean in your life?"

Narrative Discussion:

"What were the most important points of the narrative?" Discuss those points.

Reflection Question Discussion:

As you ask these questions, allow 1-2 responses for each question. They need to time to reflect and share with each other. This is a long study. They will need to build trust and community amongst each other.

30 WEEK BIBLE STUDY FOR TEEN GIRLS

"What was the hardest question to answer in the reflection questions? Why?"

"What was the most thought-provoking question in the reflection questions? Why? Did you share the question with anyone?"

"What question caused you the most concern?"

"Did you have any questions after the study? What were the questions?"

Project Discussion:

"What did you learn from the collage?"

"What did you learn about yourself from week 12?"

"What was the most important detail of your journal?"

Close with a testimony about when you God saved your reputation despite how you behaved. (Yours or an QIM.)

Answer any questions.

Next week's assignment.

Pray.

WEEK TWELVE REFLECTION

1. What was Jesus' reputation? How did you come to that summary?

   _____

   _____

2. What is your reputation? How was your reputation created/defined?

   _____

   _____

3. Do you need to improve your reputation? How can you improve your reputation? How long do you think it will take to improve it?

   _____

   _____

4. Are you the young lady that your parents want you to be? Are they proud or embarrassed about you? If that needs to be improved, how will you go about doing so?

   _____

   _____

5. Who introduced you to Christ?

   _____

   _____

6. What is your testimony? When did you accept Christ? When were you baptized? Do you share Christ with others? Whom do you share your testimony with?

   _____

7. Define leadership—your personal definition. What is God's definition of leadership? Give examples of God's definition of leadership.

8. What does your fellowship and leadership look like? Can you improve either or both? How will you do so?

9. What is your definition of image?

10. What is your image of God?

11. What is your definition of Holy?

12. What is your definition of Righteous?

13. What is your definition of forgiving/forgiveness?

14. What is your definition of love/loving?

15. What is your definition of grace?

16. What is your definition of money?

17. What is your definition of power?

18. What is your definition of wisdom?

19. What is your definition of creativity?

20. What is God's definition of image? What did He mean in Genesis 1:26-27? How close are you to that image—the likeness of God?

_____

_____

21. Is what you are doing and looking like supportive of God's desire for your image?

_____

_____

22. Is attitude part of that image? Explain.

_____

_____

23. Is God pleased with your look, your attitude, and your overall disposition?

_____

_____

24. Does God care how you look/what you wear? How do you know? What does He care about exactly?

_____

_____

25. Do you have challenges with skirt length? Do you have challenges with shirt/blouse transparency? Do you have challenges with too tight a fit? Do you have challenges with too much cleavage?

_____

_____

26. Why does your skirt have to be that short? Why can't it be long enough to cover your thigh, which leaves something to the imagination?

_____
_____

27. What message does 'short and sheer' send? What if what you meant to be sexy was actually seen as raunchy?

_____
_____

28. Do you change clothes after you leave your parent(s) presence to something you cannot wear in their presence? If so, why? Do you know what people think of your parents because of your attire?

_____
_____

29. Does your attire embarrass your family?

_____
_____

30. Share your makeup style and philosophy. Is your makeup so heavy that you look like a different person? How does it make you feel when someone does not recognize you because of your lack of makeup?

_____
_____

31. Does your hair vary so drastically that people do not recognize you? How does that make you feel?

_____
_____

32. For those who wear weave or wish to, do you NEED weave? What is wrong with the hair that God gave you?

_____

_____

33. With the hair, makeup, and clothes, who are trying to impress? What are you trying to feel better about? Why? What is the benefit of impressing them?

_____

_____

34. Are you okay with being known for this for the next 25 years? Are you okay with your daughter wearing that when she is a teenager?

_____

_____

35. What do people think of you? How do you know?

_____

_____

36. What is a good reputation? How would you maintain that good reputation? What does it take to ruin that good reputation?

_____

_____

37. How long does it take to recover from something, which damaged your reputation? What has to happen for you to recover that reputation?

_____

38. What do you say about girls who have sex and the details of their encounters have been shared? What do others say about them? Are you one of those girls that they talk about? How do you feel when you hear about these girls and their activity?

39. Why is your reputation important? Why is a good reputation important?

40. Why aren't drugs a good idea? Do you know that if you are an athlete, the team does random drug checks? Why are you seeking an altered mental state? What pain is so intense that drugs are your chosen escape path?

41. What happens when you become addicted? What is the plan for you to recover from that addiction? Who pays for that? What do you miss while you are high and while you are in recovery?

42. What does it take to say no to drugs? Do you know now to report people who offer you drugs?

43. What would influence you to drink? Where would you get alcohol from? What pain would cause you to seek this altered state?

30 WEEK BIBLE STUDY FOR TEEN GIRLS

_____

_____

44. What would you do if you were drunk and woke up the next morning, next to a stranger, naked? What would you do? What would you say? How do you find out if you had sex or not? If that sex was protected or not? What if you become pregnant? What if you were infected with a STD?

_____

_____

45. What is the plan to recover if you become addicted to alcohol? Who pays for that? What do you miss while you are drunk and in recovery?

_____

_____

46. What will be affected by that addiction? School? Family? Sports? Job/career?

_____

_____

47. How do your grades compare to your parents? Better than? About the same? Worse than?

_____

_____

48. Is it okay to be smart? Explain. If not, why not?

_____

_____

49. What can you do to avoid naked and barely clothed selfies? What would happen if a naked photo surfaced of you?

50. What would you do if your social media posts kept you off the sports team of your choice or kept you out of the college of your choice?

51. List 5 actions you can do to follow God and Jesus more closely.

52. What does following Jesus cost you?

30 WEEK BIBLE STUDY FOR TEEN GIRLS

WEEK THIRTEEN

Parents

1 Samuel 1:26-27

Matthew 19:13-14

Colossians 3:20-21

2 Samuel 2:15-25

Deuteronomy 4:9

Joel 1:31

Proverbs 23:13

Proverbs 31:28

Exodus 20:12

Proverbs 23:22

Hebrews 12:7

Leviticus 19:3

Proverbs 19:18

Proverbs 13:24

Genesis 18:19

Malachi 4:6

Ephesians 6:1-3

Joshua 24:17

Psalm 22:9

Proverbs 17:25

Psalm 112:2

Proverbs 29:17

Proverbs 17:21

1 Samuel 2:19

Proverbs 20:20

Proverbs 29:15

Read the Scripture   3 attendees

Pray   1 attendee

The Covenant of the Study   "What does covenant mean in your life?"

Narrative Discussion:

"What were the most important points of the narrative?" Discuss those points.

Reflection Question Discussion:

As you ask these questions, allow 1-2 responses for each question. They need to time to reflect and share with each other. This is a long study. They will need to build trust and community amongst each other.

"What was the hardest question to answer in the reflection questions? Why?"

"What was the most thought-provoking question in the reflection questions? Why? Did you share the question with anyone?"

"What question caused you the most concern?"

"Did you have any questions after the study? What were the questions?"

Project Discussion:

"What did you learn from writing the job descriptions?"

"What did you learn about yourself from week 13?"

"What was the most important detail of your journal?"

Close with a testimony about how you have to thank God for your parents. (Yours or an QIM.)

Answer any questions.

Next week's assignment.

Pray.

WEEK THIRTEEN REFLECTION

1. What are the expectations of your parents?

2. What do your parents expect of you? Why don't you think that those expectations are unreasonable?

3. Define love. List examples of how you demonstrate your love for your parents. List examples of how your parents demonstrate love towards you.

4. Define respect. When do you respect your parents? When do you disrespect your parents? Why?

5. Why do you have trouble listening to your parents? How do you speak to others? How do you sound to others when you speak? Would you listen to yourself when you speak? How does how you sound make you feel?

6. Do you leave others with their dignity when you speak to them? Or do they wither internally after you all part ways?

7. What kind of communicator are you going to be? How will others perceive your communication? How would you respond to you? Will you be the person everyone flocks to or flees from?

8. What makes you love them or not? What makes your love conditional? When is your love unconditional?

9. Are you thankful for having parents? Do you know other children who do not have parents? What would your life look like if you did not have parents? Or if you were not raised by your biological parents? What if you were raised by foster parents or in a group home? What if one of your parents were incarcerated or dead or both?

10. Are you grateful? Do your parents agree?

11. When was the last time your parent did something for him or herself? What do they want to do with some extra money that they would have spent on you?

30 WEEK BIBLE STUDY FOR TEEN GIRLS

12. Define trust. What does it take to gain trust? What does it take to lose trust?

_____

_____

13. Why do you act like your parents are doing something that they do not have the right to do when they discipline you? Teach you? Talk to you? Pray for you?

_____

_____

14. Define proud. Are you proud of yourself? Are your parents proud of you? Are you proud of them? What would it take for you to be proud of yourself? What would it take for you to be proud of your parents? What would it take for your parents to be proud of you?

_____

_____

15. Do you pray? Do you ever see or hear your parent(s) pray? What would your life be like if they did not pray for you? If they did not teach you, how would you learn to pray? What would you do in your time of need if you did not know how to pray?

_____

_____

16. Define fasting. Do your parents fast? Do you fast? What could you fast from other than food?

_____

_____

17. What would your parents teach you? Should your parents let the internet and school teach you everything? Summarize Deuteronomy 4:9 based on your life.

_____

18. Define obedience. Are you obedient? Why not? Reflect on Colossians 3:20-21. How can you arrange your life so that you can be obedient?

19. Summarize Malachi 4:6. How can you be closer to your parents? How can your parents be closer to you?

WEEK FOURTEEN

Ruth: Persist through what is right

Ruth 1:4, 15-18

Read the Scripture	1 attendee
Pray	1 attendee
The Covenant of the Study	"What does covenant mean in your life?"

Narrative Discussion:

"What were the most important points of the narrative?" Discuss those points.

Reflection Question Discussion:

As you ask these questions, allow 1-2 responses for each question. They need to time to reflect and share with each other. This is a long study. They will need to build trust and community amongst each other.

"What was the hardest question to answer in the reflection questions? Why?"

"What was the most thought-provoking question in the reflection questions? Why? Did you share the question with anyone?"

"What question caused you the most concern?"

"Did you have any questions after the study? What were the questions?"

Project Discussion:

"What will you help to serve at the family dinner?"

"What did you learn about yourself from week 14?"

"What was the most important detail of your journal?"

Close with a testimony about when you realized that God sent someone to watch over you on Earth. (Yours or an QIM.)

Answer any questions.

Next week's assignment.

Pray.

WEEK FOURTEEN REFLECTION

1. Define family. Who are your immediate family members?

   _____
   _____

2. Who is your favorite family member? Why?

   _____
   _____

3. What traditions does your family employ? Why those particular traditions? How long has that been a tradition? How do you contribute to that tradition?

   _____
   _____

4. What are the legacies of your family? What are you known for, for example, education, etc.? How do you fit into that legacy? What will you contribute to that legacy?

   _____
   _____

5. Based on what your family is, what will you do differently when you start your own branch of the family?

   _____
   _____

6. What do you want to change about your family?

   _____
   _____

7. What makes you proud to be in that family? What embarrasses you about your family?

_____
_____

8. What makes your family proud about you? What makes your family embarrassed about you?

_____
_____

9. What do you want to understand better about your family? Who is going to explain/share that information with you?

_____
_____

10. Are there any family secrets that you have discovered? How are you handling that?

_____
_____

11. Do you value family? On a scale of 1—10, how much? Why this number? What could increase that number? Have you shared that? What would devalue that number?

_____
_____

12. Describe your ideal family. How close is yours to your description?

_____
_____

13. What did you think of Ruth and her loyalty to Naomi? What did you learn from that situation?

30 WEEK BIBLE STUDY FOR TEEN GIRLS

_____

_____

14. Look up the word mantra. What is your family's mantra? If you don't have one, then create one.

_____

_____

WEEK FIFTEEN

Grace and Mercy Defined

Psalm 4:1

Romans 12:1

2 Samuel 24:14

1 Timothy 1:15-16

Daniel 9:18

Luke 1:50

Psalm 9:13

Nehemiah 9:31

Psalm 86:16

1 Timothy 1:2

1 Peter 2:10

Psalm 51:1

Psalm 69:16

Psalm 79:8

Romans 11:30

Read the Scripture   4 attendees

Pray   1 attendee

The Covenant of the Study   "Who will you share your covenant with?"

Narrative Discussion:

"What were the most important points of the narrative?" Discuss those points.

Reflection Question Discussion:

30 WEEK BIBLE STUDY FOR TEEN GIRLS

As you ask these questions, allow 1-2 responses for each question. They need to time to reflect and share with each other. This is a long study. They will need to build trust and community amongst each other.

"What was the hardest question to answer in the reflection questions? Why?"

"What was the most thought-provoking question in the reflection questions? Why? Did you share the question with anyone?"

"What question caused you the most concern?"

"Did you have any questions after the study? What were the questions?"

Project Discussion:

"What did you learn about grace and mercy?"

"What did you learn about yourself from week 15?"

"What was the most important detail of your journal?"

Close with a testimony about when you first understood grace and mercy. (Yours or an QIM.)

Answer any questions.

Next week's assignment.

Pray.

WEEK FIFTEEN REFLECTION

1. When have you experienced God's grace and mercy? Be specific.

_____

_____

2. How will you explain God's grace and mercy to others? How will you help them to recognize it?

_____

_____

3. When have you ignored God's grace and mercy, and still followed the wrong path?

_____

_____

4. Who has experienced grace and mercy that you have witnessed?

_____

_____

5. Who inspired you to be better as a Christian?

_____

_____

6. How will you better recognize God's grace and mercy going forward?

_____

_____

30 WEEK BIBLE STUDY FOR TEEN GIRLS

WEEK SIXTEEN

Eve: To Whom Much is Required

Genesis 2:22-25

Read the Scripture — 1 attendee

Pray — 1 attendee

The Covenant of the Study — "How will you apply covenant in your life?"

Narrative Discussion:

"What were the most important points of the narrative?" Discuss those points.

Reflection Question Discussion:

As you ask these questions, allow 1-2 responses for each question. They need to time to reflect and share with each other. This is a long study. They will need to build trust and community amongst each other.

"What was the hardest question to answer in the reflection questions? Why?"

"What was the most thought-provoking question in the reflection questions? Why? Did you share the question with anyone?"

"What question caused you the most concern?"

"Did you have any questions after the study? What were the questions?"

Project Discussion:

"What did you learn from the family meeting?"

"What did you learn about yourself from week 17?"

"What was the most important detail of your journal?"

Close with a testimony about when you first family misunderstanding. (Yours or an QIM.)

Answer any questions.

Next week's assignment.

Pray.

WEEK SIXTEEN REFLECTION

1. Who is Eve? What was expected of Eve?

   _____
   _____

2. What did Eve do wrong?

   _____
   _____

3. What was the consequence to her disobedience?

   _____
   _____

4. What is expected of you? What do your parents want for you? Why are you trying to avoid those expectations?

   _____
   _____

5. Why do you think that they are expecting too much?

   _____
   _____

6. Based on your own desires, what do you expect of yourself? How do you share those expectations with others?

   _____
   _____

7. How did you develop those self-expectations? How different are they from what your parent(s)/family expects?

_____

_____

8. What do your friends think of your expectations and your parent's expectations?

_____

_____

9. What will the world expect of you? Will you be ready to meet those expectations?

_____

_____

10. What are your daily requirements? What are your future requirements?

_____

_____

30 WEEK BIBLE STUDY FOR TEEN GIRLS

WEEK SEVENTEEN

Martha: A Bad Attitude and Wrong Motives

Luke 10:40-42 (NIV)

Read the Scripture — 1 attendee

Pray — 1 attendee

The Covenant of the Study — "What does covenant mean in your life?"

Narrative Discussion:

"What were the most important points of the narrative?" Discuss those points.

Reflection Question Discussion:

As you ask these questions, allow 1-2 responses for each question. They need to time to reflect and share with each other. This is a long study. They will need to build trust and community amongst each other.

"What was the hardest question to answer in the reflection questions? Why?"

"What was the most thought-provoking question in the reflection questions? Why? Did you share the question with anyone?"

"What question caused you the most concern?"

"Did you have any questions after the study? What were the questions?"

Project Discussion:

"What did you learn from the letters you wrote?"

"What did you learn about yourself from week 18?"

"What was the most important detail of your journal?"

Close with a testimony about when you have behaved like Martha. (Yours or an QIM.)

Answer any questions.

Next week's assignment.

Pray.

30 WEEK BIBLE STUDY FOR TEEN GIRLS

WEEK SEVENTEEN REFLECTION

1. Who is Martha to Jesus? Why does she have so much access to Jesus?

_____

_____

2. Why does Martha think that Jesus is late? If you had to grade Marth's faith, what would her grade be? Based on that grading system, how would you grade yourself?

_____

_____

3. What is your opinion of Martha? Do you relate to her or do you relate to Mary? Explain.

_____

_____

4. What would you have done when Jesus met you about the death of Lazarus? What were you expecting of Jesus? Did you understand Jesus' lesson to Martha? What was the lesson? Is there anywhere in your life that you can apply that lesson(s)?

_____

_____

5. Why was Martha so bold in her behavior and words with Jesus? Do you think that Martha should have chosen her words more carefully? Can you recall a time when you should have been quiet rather than speaking?

_____

_____

6. Do you listen to God as you should? Do you blame Jesus for your situation or your unfortunate circumstances?

_____
_____

7. What should Martha have said when Jesus arrived? What should Martha have said when Jesus wept?

_____
_____

8. What did the "late" resurrection of Lazarus teach you?

_____
_____

9. Do you consider the lessons Jesus is teaching when you have unfavorable situations? Explain.

_____
_____

10. What do you wish you could talk personally to Jesus about right now?

_____
_____

11. How do you think Martha felt when Jesus was crucified? Do you think she reflected back to those occasions? Do you think that she regretted the way she spent their time together? Do you think she wished that she could have that time back?

_____
_____

12. Do you think that Martha was selfish? Why was Martha selfish? Are you selfish? Why? Who do you know that is not selfish?

_____

_____

13. Do you question God? Not ask God questions, but do you question God?

_____

_____

14. After God shared with Martha that Mary was doing the right thing and that her motives were pure, what did Martha do (using your understanding of the text) and what should she be doing? What would you have done?

_____

_____

15. What can we do so that God is first, others are served, and our motives are pure?

_____

_____

WEEK EIGHTEEN

Naomi: Transparency and Direction

Ruth 1-4

Read the Scripture   5 attendee

Pray   1 attendee

The Covenant of the Study   "Who else is your example of covenant?"

Narrative Discussion:

"What were the most important points of the narrative?" Discuss those points.

Reflection Question Discussion:

As you ask these questions, allow 1-2 responses for each question. They need to time to reflect and share with each other. This is a long study. They will need to build trust and community amongst each other.

"What was the hardest question to answer in the reflection questions? Why?"

"What was the most thought-provoking question in the reflection questions? Why? Did you share the question with anyone?"

"What question caused you the most concern?"

"Did you have any questions after the study? What were the questions?"

Project Discussion:

"What did you learn from about yourself from Naomi?"

"What did you learn about yourself from week 18?"

"What was the most important detail of your journal?"

30 WEEK BIBLE STUDY FOR TEEN GIRLS

Close with a testimony about when you first met your Naomi. (Yours or an QIM.)

Answer any questions.

Next week's assignment.

Pray.

WEEK EIGHTEEN REFLECTION

1. Describe Naomi's characteristics. What do you admire about her (5 characteristics)? Why?

   _____

   _____

2. Do you have a mentor? A wise woman in your life in addition to your family?

   _____

   _____

3. Who mentors you? Invests in you? Shares wisdom with you?

   _____

   _____

4. Who knows your dreams? Goals? Aspirations? What are they doing to help you to reach and to achieve those dreams, goals and aspirations?

   _____

   _____

5. Who gives you direction and advice? Who is ideal to do that?

   _____

   _____

6. Are you aware of the sacrifice required to help you?

   _____

   _____

30 WEEK BIBLE STUDY FOR TEEN GIRLS

7. Are you cooperative and compliant? Receptive? Obedient? Pleasant to help?

_____

_____

8. Are you worth helping? Why?

_____

_____

9. Are there times when you are hard to help? When do you not listen?

_____

_____

WEEK NINETEEN

Esther: Overcoming Your Position

Esther 1-9

Read the Scripture											1 attendee

Pray												1 attendee

The Covenant of the Study				"What does covenant mean in your life?"

Narrative Discussion:

"What were the most important points of the narrative?" Discuss those points.

Reflection Question Discussion:

As you ask these questions, allow 1-2 responses for each question. They need to time to reflect and share with each other. This is a long study. They will need to build trust and community amongst each other.

"What was the hardest question to answer in the reflection questions? Why?"

"What was the most thought-provoking question in the reflection questions? Why? Did you share the question with anyone?"

"What question caused you the most concern?"

"Did you have any questions after the study? What were the questions?"

Project Discussion:

"What did you learn from the affirmation which you wrote?"

"What did you learn about yourself from week 19?"

"What was the most important detail of your journal?"

30 WEEK BIBLE STUDY FOR TEEN GIRLS

Close with a testimony about when you first understood the role of a mentor in your life. (Yours or an QIM.)

Answer any questions.

Next week's assignment.

Pray.

WEEK NINETEEN REFLECTION

1. What is your opinion of Esther? What would you have done if you grew up in her time? Do you realize that she is your age?

___

2. What do you want to do that seems overcome with obstacles? How will you overcome those obstacles? Who will you need to help you to overcome those obstacles?

___

3. What does Esther do that you should emulate? Why?

___

4. What do you admire about Esther? Why?

___

5. How does it feel to be chosen? How does it feel to achieve what you have been chosen to do?

___

6. Do you know what you dream of? What does it take to achieve those dreams? Who do you know that has done those things? When will you contact them to get their advice about your dream?

___

30 WEEK BIBLE STUDY FOR TEEN GIRLS

_____

7. For whom do you take a stand? Why? Who takes a stand for you? Why?

_____

_____

8. What are you concerned about? What is on your mind consistently?

_____

_____

9. Who does God want you to help? Take a stand for? Why?

_____

_____

10. Could you have been Esther? What can you do that resembles Esther's care and concern? What do you care about? What concerns you? What do you care about? What concerns you? Can you help bring back a culture which has faltered? What are you willing to do? What will you do?

_____

_____

WEEK TWENTY

Hannah: A Prayer Warrior

Transparent and Unwavering

1 Samuel 1-2

Read the Scripture   5 attendees

Pray   1 attendee

The Covenant of the Study   "What does Hannah do to exemplify covenant?"

Narrative Discussion:

"What were the most important points of the narrative?" Discuss those points.

Reflection Question Discussion:

As you ask these questions, allow 1-2 responses for each question. They need to time to reflect and share with each other. This is a long study. They will need to build trust and community amongst each other.

"What was the hardest question to answer in the reflection questions? Why?"

"What was the most thought-provoking question in the reflection questions? Why? Did you share the question with anyone?"

"What question caused you the most concern?"

"Did you have any questions after the study? What were the questions?"

Project Discussion:

"What did you learn from Hannah's prayers?"

30 WEEK BIBLE STUDY FOR TEEN GIRLS

"What did you learn about yourself from week 20?"

"What was the most important detail of your journal?"

Close with a testimony about when you first prayed authentically to God. (Yours or an QIM.)

Answer any questions.

Next week's assignment.

Pray.

WEEK TWENTY REFLECTION

1. What is most impressive about Hannah? What will you do in your life based on what Hannah shows you?

   _____

   _____

2. What was powerful about the prayer that Hannah prayed?

   _____

   _____

3. Could you have kept the promise that Hannah made and kept? Why or why not? If not, what will you do so that you can keep your word and fulfill your promises?

   _____

   _____

4. Do you pray? What happens when you pray? Do you have an example of when God has answered your prayer(s)?

   _____

   _____

5. What makes you not pray? What makes you afraid to pray? Whom do you know who prays consistently?

   _____

   _____

6. What do you think is worthy of prayer? What is not worthy of prayer?

   _____

   _____

30 WEEK BIBLE STUDY FOR TEEN GIRLS

7. How do you make decisions when you don't pray?

_____

_____

8. Whom will you pray with? When will you pray? What will you pray about?

_____

_____

9. Whom will you share your prayer life with?

_____

_____

10. Are you able to help others pray?

_____

_____

WEEK TWENTY-ONE

Bathsheba

Situational Sin: When Your Plan to Sin Fails

2 Samuel 11—12

Read the Scripture	5 attendees
Pray	1 attendee
The Covenant of the Study	"What does sin do to interrupt the covenant you have with God?"

Narrative Discussion:

"What were the most important points of the narrative?" Discuss those points.

Reflection Question Discussion:

As you ask these questions, allow 1-2 responses for each question. They need to time to reflect and share with each other. This is a long study. They will need to build trust and community amongst each other.

"What was the hardest question to answer in the reflection questions? Why?"

"What was the most thought-provoking question in the reflection questions? Why? Did you share the question with anyone?"

"What question caused you the most concern?"

"Did you have any questions after the study? What were the questions?"

Project Discussion:

"What did you learn from Bathsheba's situation?"

30 WEEK BIBLE STUDY FOR TEEN GIRLS

"What did you learn about yourself from week 21?"

"What was the most important detail of your journal?"

Close with a testimony about when you felt the wrath of God because of God. (Yours or an QIM.)

Answer any questions.

Next week's assignment.

Pray.

WEEK TWENTY-ONE REFLECTION

1. What are your sins?

   _____

   _____

2. What entices you to sin?

   _____

   _____

3. What events or details stop you from sinning?

   _____

   _____

4. Who gets you in the most trouble? Who do you cause to sin?

   _____

   _____

5. What will it take for you to stop sinning?

   _____

   _____

6. Do you ask God for help to stop? Consistently?

   _____

   _____

7. What was your opinion of Bathsheba because of her sins?

30 WEEK BIBLE STUDY FOR TEEN GIRLS

_____

_____

8. What was your opinion of David because of his sins?

_____

_____

9. As Bathsheba, what could she have done differently to avoid the situation?

_____

_____

10. Who was punished because someone else was punished?

_____

_____

WEEK TWENTY-TWO

Lois and Eunice: A Legacy of Faith

2 Timothy 1:5

Read the Scripture   1 attendee

Pray   1 attendee

The Covenant of the Study   "What does covenant mean in your life?"

Narrative Discussion:

"What were the most important points of the narrative?" Discuss those points.

Reflection Question Discussion:

As you ask these questions, allow 1-2 responses for each question. They need to time to reflect and share with each other. This is a long study. They will need to build trust and community amongst each other.

"What was the hardest question to answer in the reflection questions? Why?"

"What was the most thought-provoking question in the reflection questions? Why? Did you share the question with anyone?"

"What question caused you the most concern?"

"Did you have any questions after the study? What were the questions?"

Project Discussion:

"What did you learn from Eunice and Lois?"

"What did you learn about yourself from week 22?"

"What was the most important detail of your journal?"

30 WEEK BIBLE STUDY FOR TEEN GIRLS

Close with a testimony about when your faith was challenged. (Yours or an QIM.)

Answer any questions.

Next week's assignment.

Pray.

WEEK TWENTY-TWO

1. How do you define faith?

2. Who has faith that you respect? What does that faith look like?

3. How do others share their faith with you?

4. When was his/her faith made evident to you?

5. What does faith mean to you?

6. Do others know that you have faith? How do they know?

7. Are there events which caused you to question God? Explain. Or get close to questioning God? Doubt God? Disbelieve in God? Explain.

_____

_____

8. What do you want God to give you that He has not yet given you? Can you live without that?

_____

_____

9. Will you continue to love God and serve God regardless of your circumstances?

_____

_____

10. Can you still believe in God and believe God when seemingly the worst has happened?

_____

_____

11. Have you ever asked God 'why is this happening to me?' What did God say? How did that make you feel? What are you going to do if God says 'why not you?'

_____

_____

12. What will it take for you to have great faith?

_____

_____

13. How would you grade your faith on a scale of 1-10, 10 being the best? What can you do to improve that number?

_____

_____

30 WEEK BIBLE STUDY FOR TEEN GIRLS

WEEK TWENTY-THREE

Lydia: Being First Has Its Benefits

Sharing Jesus With Others

Acts 16:11-15

Read the Scripture	1 attendee
Pray	1 attendee
The Covenant of the Study	"What did covenant mean to Lydia?"

Narrative Discussion:

"What were the most important points of the narrative?" Discuss those points.

Reflection Question Discussion:

As you ask these questions, allow 1-2 responses for each question. They need to time to reflect and share with each other. This is a long study. They will need to build trust and community amongst each other.

"What was the hardest question to answer in the reflection questions? Why?"

"What was the most thought-provoking question in the reflection questions? Why? Did you share the question with anyone?"

"What question caused you the most concern?"

"Did you have any questions after the study? What were the questions?"

Project Discussion:

"What did you learn from Lydia's testimony? Did her testimony ignite your zeal for God?"

"What did you learn about yourself from week 23?"

"What was the most important detail of your journal?"

Close with a testimony about when you shared God with others. (Yours or an QIM.)

Answer any questions.

Next week's assignment.

Pray.

WEEK TWENTY-THREE REFLECTION

1. Who is responsible for you knowing Christ and God?

_____

_____

2. When did you first hear about God?

_____

_____

3. How would you know about God if you were never invited to church or someone never shared God with you?

_____

_____

4. Was your family involved in your conversion? Explain. Are they converted as well?

_____

_____

5. What did you do next after the conversion? Did you share your conversion with your family?

_____

_____

6. Did you share your conversion with your friends? How? What was their reaction?

_____

_____

7. Are you obedient and brave enough to share Jesus with others? What will it take to share Jesus with others?

_____

_____

8. What does Lydia do that inspires you to share Jesus?

_____

_____

9. What is the scariest part of sharing? What are you afraid of?

_____

_____

10. If you don't share when you are designed to share, then how will they learn of Jesus? Who will God assign in your spot?

_____

_____

11. How do you think you will know you need to share?

_____

_____

30 WEEK BIBLE STUDY FOR TEEN GIRLS

WEEK TWENTY-FOUR

Mary: A Life Worthy of Being Called

Luke 1:26-56, 2

Read the Scripture

Pray

The Covenant of the Study

5 attendees

1 attendee

"How does Mary elevate the definition of covenant?"

Narrative Discussion:

"What were the most important points of the narrative?" Discuss those points.

Reflection Question Discussion:

As you ask these questions, allow 1-2 responses for each question. They need to time to reflect and share with each other. This is a long study. They will need to build trust and community amongst each other.

"What was the hardest question to answer in the reflection questions? Why?"

"What was the most thought-provoking question in the reflection questions? Why? Did you share the question with anyone?"

"What question caused you the most concern?"

"Did you have any questions after the study? What were the questions?"

Project Discussion:

"What did you learn from Mary?"

"What did you learn about yourself from week 24?"

"What was the most important detail of your journal?"

Close with a testimony about when you thought about Mary being the mother of Jesus and then Him being her Lord. (Yours or an QIM.)

Answer any questions.

Next week's assignment.

Pray.

WEEK TWENTY-FOUR REFLECTION

1. What would have been your reaction if you had been Mary? What is our opinion of Mary?

   _____
   _____

2. What do you want God to choose you for?

   _____
   _____

3. What do you think God has chosen you for?

   _____
   _____

4. What are you doing that you never imagined you would?

   _____
   _____

5. What do you need to do to correct aspects of your life which challenges your ability to be chosen?

   _____
   _____

6. What has He chosen you for which you are trying to avoid?

   _____
   _____

7. What do you need to modify so that you can hear from God?

_____

_____

8. What do you need to alter so that you can see the hand of God?

_____

_____

9. Can God trust you to do His work according to His will? What will it take for you to arrive there?

_____

_____

10. What has God already done in your life which makes you resemble and/or feel like Mary?

_____

_____

30 WEEK BIBLE STUDY FOR TEEN GIRLS

WEEK TWENTY-FIVE

The Issue of Blood:

A Dogmatic Perseverance and Without the Issue of Image

Luke 8:42b-48

Read the Scripture	1 attendee
Pray	1 attendee
The Covenant of the Study	"What happens when you realize that covenant was absent but now necessary?"

Narrative Discussion:

"What were the most important points of the narrative?" Discuss those points.

Reflection Question Discussion:

As you ask these questions, allow 1-2 responses for each question. They need to time to reflect and share with each other. This is a long study. They will need to build trust and community amongst each other.

"What was the hardest question to answer in the reflection questions? Why?"

"What was the most thought-provoking question in the reflection questions? Why? Did you share the question with anyone?"

"What question caused you the most concern?"

"Did you have any questions after the study? What were the questions?"

Project Discussion:

"What did you learn from the woman? Did you admire her?"

"What did you learn about yourself from week 25?"

"What was the most important detail of your journal?"

Close with a testimony about when you wanted God at this level. (Yours or an QIM.)

Answer any questions.

Next week's assignment.

Pray.

WEEK TWENTY-FIVE REFLECTION

1. What is your opinion of this woman? How would you handle her situation if it were yours?

   _____

   _____

2. How would you feel? Scared? Overwhelmed? Distraught? Peaceful? Calm? Courageous?

   _____

   _____

3. What numerical value would you assign to her faith? How does it compare to yours?

   _____

   _____

4. What can you do that is outrageous and outlandish which demonstrates your faith in God, Jesus and the Holy Spirit?

   _____

   _____

5. What is your 'issue of blood'? Family? Health? Grades? Social? Future? Relationships?

   _____

   _____

6. What does Jesus want/expect for you to do about your 'issue'? What are going to do?

   _____

   _____

7. Whom are you going to ask to pray with you? Whom are you going to tell when your 'issue' is solved?

_____

_____

8. What did she inspire you to do/achieve/attempt?

_____

_____

9. How did your connection to Jesus increase once reading what He did?

_____

_____

10. What will He do for you based on what He did for her?

_____

_____

11. What would you have done after the healing?

_____

_____

30 WEEK BIBLE STUDY FOR TEEN GIRLS

WEEK TWENTY-SIX

Work Ethic

Colossians 3:23

Read the Scripture — 1 attendee

Pray — 1 attendee

The Covenant of the Study — "What does covenant mean in your life?"

Narrative Discussion:

"What were the most important points of the narrative?" Discuss those points.

Reflection Question Discussion:

As you ask these questions, allow 1-2 responses for each question. They need to time to reflect and share with each other. This is a long study. They will need to build trust and community amongst each other.

"What was the hardest question to answer in the reflection questions? Why?"

"What was the most thought-provoking question in the reflection questions? Why? Did you share the question with anyone?"

"What question caused you the most concern?"

"Did you have any questions after the study? What were the questions?"

Project Discussion:

"With whom will you share your vision board?"

"What did you learn about yourself from week 26?"

"What was the most important detail of your journal?"

Close with a testimony about when God met your desires in an unbelievable way. (Yours or an QIM.)

Answer any questions.

Next week's assignment.

Pray.

WEEK TWENTY-SIX REFLECTION

1. What have you done today to invest in your future? If nothing, why not?

_____

_____

2. Define work ethic. Who taught you the work ethic that you have?

_____

_____

3. Are you a good student? Why or why not?

_____

_____

4. What do your teachers think of you? How do you know? Is that real or perceived? Based on what specific situations?

_____

_____

5. Do you know that they judge who you are based on what you produce in their classroom? Do you know that they judge who you are going to be based on the work that you produce in their classroom? Is it fair that you are judged by the work that you produce? What should you be judged on?

_____

_____

6. How do you define work ethic? What does it mean to you? How would grade your work ethic?

_____

7. Who has the best work ethic that you know? What did they do to make you pay attention to their work ethic? What are you going to do to impress them with yours?

_____

_____

8. Do you feel prepared to be successful in the world? What does it take to reach that in your life?

_____

_____

9. Why is work ethic important? What does it mean to you? How will you improve your attitude?

_____

_____

10. Do your teachers feel that you have work ethic, which they could support publicly? Does your family feel that way about you? Do you feel that way about yourself?

_____

_____

30 WEEK BIBLE STUDY FOR TEEN GIRLS

WEEK TWENTY-SEVEN

With Zeal, Pursue and Proceed

Revelation 3:16

Philippians 4:13

James 1:2-4

Read the Scripture   3 attendees

Pray   1 attendee

The Covenant of the Study   "What does covenant mean in the life of your friends and family?"

Narrative Discussion:

"What were the most important points of the narrative?" Discuss those points.

Reflection Question Discussion:

As you ask these questions, allow 1-2 responses for each question. They need to time to reflect and share with each other. This is a long study. They will need to build trust and community amongst each other.

"What was the hardest question to answer in the reflection questions? Why?"

"What was the most thought-provoking question in the reflection questions? Why? Did you share the question with anyone?"

"What question caused you the most concern?"

"Did you have any questions after the study? What were the questions?"

Project Discussion:

"What did you learn from the questions you asked from your family members?"

"What did you learn about yourself from week 27?"

"What was the most important detail of your journal?"

Close with a testimony about when you pursued God with zeal. (Yours or an QIM.)

Answer any questions.

Next week's assignment.

Pray.

WEEK TWENTY-SEVEN REFLECTION

1. How would you grade your current effort in your life? Scale 1 to 10; 10 being the best.

   _____

   _____

2. Are you satisfied with that level? If not, what needs to happen so that you can be satisfied?

   _____

   _____

3. What will you do?

   _____

   _____

4. What does it mean to you to pursue a life of excellence?

   _____

   _____

5. Where do you want your life to go? Goals: name them.

   _____

   _____

6. What college/university would you like to attend? What are the admission requirements? (Hint: go to the school's website, the admissions tab)

   _____

   _____

7. What are you afraid of? Can that stop you from pursuing a life of excellence? What can we do to prevent that?

_____

_____

8. Who are you when no one is watching and what will you do when those who you are accountable for you are not present or seemingly not watching? Who are you when you are out front or on stage or being watched?

_____

_____

9. What do you avoid but should do? Why do you have an attitude—you reject the request in your heart—when your parents ask you to do anything? Why aren't you willing to participate in our life?

_____

_____

10. Your best future: what do you dream of? What career have you always talked about? What do you want to do to help others? What is your dream life? What does it take to achieve that? Why do you want it? What are you willing to do to get it?

_____

_____

11. If you are not hot, passionate, zealous, excited, determined, enthusiastic, or driven for yourself then nobody will believe that you will invest in anything else at a higher level. Do you think so? Do you agree? So if you don't feel that you should be zealous, determined, driven about your life, then why not?

_____

_____

12. What have you done today to invest in your future?

30 WEEK BIBLE STUDY FOR TEEN GIRLS

_____

_____

13. Is God pleased with the attitude of someone He created in His image? Is He pleased with your attitude? Final note: your parent had a bad day too but manages to ask you about yours in a caring and pleasant manner. Could you respond in a warm, caring and pleasant manner? When you are having the worst day, can you say 'can I have a few minutes/hours/days to respond to that?' rather than have a horrible reaction? What does it take to fix your attitude?

_____

_____

WEEK TWENTY-EIGHT

Weapons for Warfare

Ephesians 6:10-18

Read the Scripture	2 attendees
Pray	1 attendee
The Covenant of the Study	"What does covenant mean in your life?"

Narrative Discussion:

"What were the most important points of the narrative?" Discuss those points.

Reflection Question Discussion:

As you ask these questions, allow 1-2 responses for each question. They need to time to reflect and share with each other. This is a long study. They will need to build trust and community amongst each other.

"What was the hardest question to answer in the reflection questions? Why?"

"What was the most thought-provoking question in the reflection questions? Why? Did you share the question with anyone?"

"What question caused you the most concern?"

"Did you have any questions after the study? What were the questions?"

Project Discussion:

"What did you learn from the description of the weapons?"

30 WEEK BIBLE STUDY FOR TEEN GIRLS

"What did you learn about yourself from week 28?"

"What was the most important detail of your journal?"

Close with a testimony about when you use those weapons for God. (Yours or an QIM.)

Answer any questions.

Next week's assignment.

Pray.

WEEK TWENTY-EIGHT REFLECTION

1. What did you consider a weapon before these scriptures? Whom did you think we were fighting?

_____
_____

2. How will these scriptures help you to fight now? How do you share these concepts with others?

_____
_____

3. How will you change your "bad" behaviors (for example: messy, liar, etc.)?

_____
_____

4. Do you ever let the devil use you without your knowledge? With your knowledge? Explain.

_____
_____

5. What area(s) do you need to improve upon? How will you do that?

_____
_____

30 WEEK BIBLE STUDY FOR TEEN GIRLS

WEEK TWENTY-NINE

God Made You a Girl

Proverbs 31:10—31

Read the Scripture	4 attendees
Pray	1 attendee
The Covenant of the Study	"What does covenant mean in your life?"

Narrative Discussion:

"What were the most important points of the narrative?" Discuss those points.

Reflection Question Discussion:

As you ask these questions, allow 1-2 responses for each question. They need to time to reflect and share with each other. This is a long study. They will need to build trust and community amongst each other.

"What was the hardest question to answer in the reflection questions? Why?"

"What was the most thought-provoking question in the reflection questions? Why? Did you share the question with anyone?"

"What question caused you the most concern?"

"Did you have any questions after the study? What were the questions?"

Project Discussion:

"What did you learn from this ideal woman?"

"What did you learn about yourself from week 29?"

"What was the most important detail of your journal?"

Close with a testimony about when you first knew what the definition of a woman according to God's definition. (Yours or an QIM.)

Answer any questions.

Next week's assignment.

Pray.

WEEK TWENTY-NINE REFLECTION

1. What is your definition of yourself as a girl? How closely aligned is that to God's definition?
___
___

2. Which scriptures will you apply to your life within 30 days?
___
___

3. 90 days?
___
___

4. 6 months?
___
___

5. One year?
___
___

6. Five years?
___
___

7. Ten years?

_____

_____

30 WEEK BIBLE STUDY FOR TEEN GIRLS

WEEK THIRTY

Today Affects Tomorrow

Proverbs 31:10—31

Read the Scripture — 1 attendee

Pray — 1 attendee

The Covenant of the Study — "What does covenant mean in your life?

Does it mean more now than it did before?"

Narrative Discussion:

"What were the most important points of the narrative?" Discuss those points.

Reflection Question Discussion:

As you ask these questions, allow 1-2 responses for each question. They need to time to reflect and share with each other. This is a long study. They will need to build trust and community amongst each other.

"What was the hardest question to answer in the reflection questions? Why?"

"What was the most thought-provoking question in the reflection questions? Why? Did you share the question with anyone?"

"What question caused you the most concern?"

"Did you have any questions after the study? What were the questions?"

Project Discussion:

"What did you learn about the cost of your sin?"

"What did you learn about yourself from week 30?"

"What was the most important detail of your journal?"

Close with a testimony about when you understood the cost of your sins. (Yours or an QIM.)

Answer any questions.

Next week's assignment.

Pray.

WEEK THIRTY REFLECTION

1. Share your thoughts about woman 1. What would you do differently? What would you do instead?

   _____

   _____

2. Share your thoughts about woman 2. What would you do differently? What would you do instead?

   _____

   _____

3. Share your thoughts about woman 3. What would you do differently? What would you do instead?

   _____

   _____

4. Share your thoughts about woman 4. What would you do differently? What would you do instead?

   _____

   _____

5. Share your thoughts about woman 5. What would you do differently? What would you do instead?

   _____

   _____

6. Share your thoughts about woman 6. What would you do differently? What would you do instead?

   _____

   _____

Queen in the Making

7. What will you do when presented with the concept of sex? Will you say yes? If you already said yes, did you regret it?

_____

_____

8. How will you recover from a failed relationship where sex was involved?

_____

_____

9. Why try drugs? How can you become strong enough to say no? What happens when you become addicted? What if you die from the use of the drug?

_____

_____

10. What if you are unable to play sports or do other activities because you failed a drug test? Do you know that careers do random drug tests on their employees? The results could be your loss of employment. Can you afford to lose your job due to drug usage?

_____

_____

11. Do you know that drug charges (because of possession) will prevent you from receiving financial aid? How will you pay for school?

_____

_____

12. What happens if the drugs cause your organs to shut down? Research the effects of drug use.

_____

_____

13. Have you ever considered suicide? Why? Have you told your parent(s)? How would you commit suicide if you attempted?

14. Do you cut yourself? Do you know what cutting is? Do you know that those scars can be permanent?

15. What can we do to help you feel better about yourself?

16. How would your parents and friends feel if you killed yourself?

Resources

www.onediagage.com

War Room (movie)

Akeelah and the Bee (movie)

Coach Carter (movie)

The Hive (movie)

As We Grow Together Daily Devotional for Expectant Couples

As We Grow Together Prayer Journal for Expectant Couples

The Blue Print: Poetry for the Soul

From Two to One: The Notebook for Couples

In Purple Ink: Poetry for the Spirit

Living a Whole Life: Sermons which Prompt, Provoke and Promote Life

Love Letters to God from a Teenage Girl

The Measure of a Woman: The Details of Her Soul

The Notebook: For Me, About Me, By Me

The Notebook for the Christian Teen

On This Journey Daily Devotional for Young People

On This Journey Prayer Journal for Young People

30 WEEK BIBLE STUDY FOR TEEN GIRLS

One Day More Than We Deserve Daily Devotional for the Growing Christian

One Day More Than We Deserve Prayer Journal for the Growing Christian

Promises, Promises: A Christian Novel

Tools for These Times: Timely Sermons for Uncertain Times

With An Anointed Voice: The Power of Prayer

Yielded and Submitted: A Woman's Journey for a Life Dedicated to God

Yielded and Submitted: A Woman's Journey for a Life Dedicated to God Prayers and Journal

Yielded and Submitted: A Woman's Journey for a Life Dedicated to God An Intimate Study

The Power of a Praying Woman Stormie Omartian

The Power of a Praying Wife Stormie Omartian

Discerning the Voice of God Priscilla Shirer

Kingdom Woman Tony Evans and Crystal Evans Hurst

ACKNOWLEDGEMENTS

God, thank You for Your plans for me. Thank You for **Queen in the Making 30 Week Bible Study for Teen Girls** and choosing me to complete Your project. I just want to please You. Thank You for continuing to anoint me and to invest in me and my gifts, which keep surprising me. Thank You for loving and forgiving me.

Hillary and Nehemiah, thank you for supporting me and my endeavors. Thank you for loving me, especially when I do nothing without a pen and a clipboard, thank you for enduring my late nights, your ideas, the sounding board, the love and the support. Thank you for celebrating our legacy.

Kimberly 'Ann' Joiner, thank you for reading my work and offering your honest feedback. May your life be blessed for doing God's will.

To the girls who have raised their hands in need of this study. I don't know all of you, but the ones I do know, I apologize. I got it to you as quickly as I could. I love you!

To my prayer partners and to my accountability partners, thank you for the long talks and the powerful prayers and the encouragement. To my pastor and church family, thank you so much for your love and support.

30 WEEK BIBLE STUDY FOR TEEN GIRLS

Minister Onedia N. Gage seeks to share her outlandish pursuit of God with her prayers, study and meditation. She desires to share her faith in a manner which helps you do the same through her calling. She hopes that these words bless you.

Please feel free to contact and share your testimony. onediagage@onediagage.com, or @onediangage (twitter). www.onediagage.com

Blogtalkradio.com/onediagage

Youtube.com/onediagage

Facebook.com/onedia-gage-ministries

30 WEEK BIBLE STUDY FOR TEEN GIRLS

PREACHER ♦ ADVOCATE ♦ TEACHER ♦ FACILITATOR
CONFERENCE SPEAKER ♦ WORKSHOP LEADER

To invite Rev. Gage to speak to the teens at your church, women's ministry,

The full congregation or any other ministry.

Please contact us at: www.onedigage.com

@onediangage (twitter) ♦ onediagage@onediagage.com ♦ facebook.com/onediagageministries

youtube.com/onediagage ♦ blogtalkradio.com/onediagage ♦ ongage (Instagram)

30 WEEK BIBLE STUDY FOR TEEN GIRLS

Publishing

Do you have a book you want to write, but do not know what to do?

Do you have a book you need to publish but do not know how to start?

Would publishing move your career forward?

Let us help

onediagage@purpleink.net ♦ www.purpleink.net

281.740.5143 ♦ 512.715.4243